D1513072

NATIONAL
GALLERY

George Stubbs, 1724–1806
Whistlejacket, about 1762
© The National Gallery, London

Georges Seurat, 1859–1891
Bathers at Asnières, 1884
© The National Gallery, London

NATIONAL
GALLERY

Johannes Vermeer, 1632–1675
A Young Woman standing at a Virginal, about 1670–2
© The National Gallery, London

Thomas Gainsborough, 1727–1788
Mr and Mrs Andrews, about 1750
© The National Gallery, London